THE NINE PEBBLES

LIFE THROUGH POETRY

AJAY ADALA

INDIA • SINGAPORE • MALAYSIA

ISBN 979-8-88749-862-1

CONTENTS

ACKNOWLEDGMENT

I would like to thank my wife Keerti Chandana, my son Advith, and my daughter Seshasayani, for showing immense patience and cooperation while writing these heart-felt poems. They created a positive environment at home which went a long way in helping me complete the nine poems. I would also like to thank my friends for their timely review of poems and good suggestions.

I thank my publisher, M/s Notion Press, for agreeing to publish the poems in the form of a book.

PREFACE

"The Nine Pebbles" is a collection of nine poems. It is a well-known fact that pebbles are just stones that are subjected to rubbing and polishing by flowing water. In this process, the pebbles look much more gracious than in their original form. Similarly, the poems written in this book are a result of intense learning gained during implementation of electronic governance (e-Governance) projects. The poems cover a wide range of subjects including nature, software, personal living, government, etc. The objective of writing the poems is to make readers involved in the subject and try to connect in the best manner based on their situation.

I hope the poems make your life lighter and ensure smooth living.

PEBBLE 1: MY COUNTRY, OUR WORLD

The poem involves various aspects of life, events, natural calamities, governance, anti-social activities, and other attributes. The poem does not restrict to a single country and describes events that may apply to other countries also. Through the poem, the reader is informed about the appropriate way to handle each such event with good intention. The purpose of the poem is to address events in a positive manner and ensure all countries are green and humane.

MY COUNTRY, OUR WORLD

Born, Raised, Trained, Educated,

One Country or several in the World effected,

I thank the Country whole-hearted.

Mountain, Forest, Desert, Cultivated,

One Country or several in the World existed,

I protect nature care-hearted.

Religion, Culture, Tradition, Connected,

One Country or several in World adopted,

I respect the practice kind-hearted.

Democracy, Authoritarian, Monarchy, Dictated,

One Country or several in the World administrated,

I live with the administration warm-hearted.

Academics, Sports, Cultural, Concerted,

One Country or several in World promoted,

I cheer the achievers good-hearted.

Virus, Earthquake, Tsunami, Destructed,
One Country or several in World affected,
I help the suffered humane-hearted.

Terror, Hostility, Discrimination, Assaulted,
One Country or several in World confronted,
I address the cause open-hearted.

Unmannered, Revengeful, Unethical, Corrupted,
One Country or several in World tainted,
I transform the behavior clean-hearted.

Finally, it is my Country and our World undoubted,
I give my heart to make it green and humane persisted,
To ensure life with peace and harmony ever-lasted.

PEBBLE 2: WE VOTE

The poem describes situations that prevail before voting (at the time of campaigning) and after voting (after the declaration of the result). The poem appreciates citizens for exercising their vote. The purpose of the poem is to bring about a change in the manner elections are contested. The underlying intention is to ensure that situations before voting and after voting do not vary substantially.

WE VOTE

Mean a lot before voting,
Lean a lot after voting,
We still vote, not by compulsion,
But to gain inclusion.

Promises before voting,
Compromises after voting,
We still vote, not by calculation,
But to keep up the competition.

The hype before voting,
The hope after voting,
We still vote, not by expectation,
But to see good implementation.

Plenty of candidates before voting,
No sight of candidate after voting,
We still vote, not by intuition,
But to ensure the right selection.

Door-to-door campaign before voting,
Never at the door after voting,
We still vote, not by assurance,
But to expect reassurance.

Gush of speeches before voting,
Hardly any speech after voting,
We still vote, not by voice,
But to exercise choice.

Blame game before voting,
Name game after voting,
We still vote, not by might,
But to keep our right.

Fine color before voting,
True color after voting,
We still vote, not by anticipation,
But to hope for transformation.

Finally, who am I before voting,
What I become after voting,
We still vote, not by pity,
But to prove our identity.

PEBBLE 3: THE BUDGET

The poem tries to explain the concept of the government budget and how the government treasury operates. It is a known fact that the details of how the government treasury operates are only explained in the form of Acts, Rules, and Codes and are not available as a curriculum in any educational course. I had an opportunity to work as a consultant to the Department of Treasuries for a brief period during which I learned the various aspects including Head of Account, Revenue, Expenditure, and DDOs. The purpose of the poem is to give an understanding of the basic operation of the government treasury and the underlying objective of the government budget.

THE BUDGET

Government Budget, a concept to explain,
Though its understanding involves a bit of pain,
With little experience, I like it to be elaborated,
The bits and pieces that give meaning when consolidated.

Money for a Scheme is allocated in the "Head of Account",
Similar to money parked in a Bank Account,
Government operates Hundreds of Head of Accounts,
Treasury maintains the status of these Accounts.

Receipts and Payments are always segregated,
They have separate Head of Accounts to be accounted,
Revenue Head of Accounts only to receive money,
Expenditure Head of Accounts only to spend money.

Taxes, Duties, Grants, and Cess are taken as revenue,
Loans, Bonds, and Funds are treated similar to revenue,
All are deposited in the Revenue Head of Accounts,
For calculating deficit with Expenditure Head of Accounts.

Bills, Invoices, and Advances are processed as payments,
Can be internal payments or external payments,
Internal payments involve transfer to Head of Accounts,
External payments involve transfers to Bank Accounts.

The procedure to draw money by an Officer,
It is only by DDO (Drawing and Disbursement Officer),
Prepare and submit Bills to Treasury,
For scrutiny and release of payments to the beneficiary.

The budget aims to enhance revenue to Government,
By change in taxes, production, investment, divestment,
The focus is to increase goods and services production,
By providing an environment near to perfection.

The more the revenue to Government,
The higher the expenditure by Government,
The larger the Programs or Schemes in variety,
The greater the benefits to society.

The budget has an impact on the economy of a nation,
With an aim to never allow it to be in stagnation,
The goal is to ensure the development of States in unison,
With a spirit of uniformity, equality, and comparison.

PEBBLE 4: I BREATHE AND LIVE

The poem tries to bring out various situations encountered in different stages of life. These stages include new-born, child, adolescent, graduate, professional, mid-career, family, retirement, etc. A person undergoes unrest and tension depending on the situation. The purpose of the poem is to motivate and strengthen the reader to continue living, whatever the status, with a hope to achieve success.

I BREATHE AND LIVE

The cry when I am born,
Inabilities all around adorn,
Wait for a drop of milk to flow,
Still, I breathe and live with a hope to glow.

The rules when I am a child,
Situations make it stern or mild,
Hurdles never seem to end,
Still, I breathe and live with a hope to defend.

The nascence when I am an adolescent,
Failures reflecting past and present,
Plenty to observe and learn,
Still, I breathe and live with a hope to yearn.

The turbulence when I am a graduate,
Differences which seem to fluctuate,
Choices in habits, culture, and temper,
Still, I breathe and live with a hope to prosper.

The stress when I am a professional,

Plenty of compromises turn emotional,

Concern to share time with family, work, friend,

Still, I breathe and live with a hope to trend.

The uncertainty when I am in relation,

Unbearable pain in rejection or separation,

Attempt to make it green and high-end,

Still, I breathe and live with a hope to mend.

The struggle when I am married,

Worries and depression varied,

Whom to listen, spouse or parent,

Still, I breathe and live with a hope to be patient.

The crisis when in mid-career,

Desperate to find solutions to steer,

Sense pressure from all over,

Still, I breathe and live with a hope to cross over.

The tension when I am unwell,

Always in a hurry to get well,

Never wanted to lose health with age,

Still, I breathe and live with a hope to manage.

The fear when I am stuck in terror,

Always question whose error,

Finding ways and means to survive,

Still, I breathe and live with a hope to revive.

The confusion when I retire,

Doubts on energy left to respire,

The unsolved puzzle, whether to work or rest,

Still, I breathe and live with a hope to be the best.

The cry when I am dying,

Inabilities all around flying,

Wait for a drop of energy to flow,

Still, I breathe and live with a hope to slow.

PEBBLE 5: RELIGION

The poem attempts to handle a sensitive subject (religion) and tries to analyze its various aspects. These include the need for religion, change of religion, insult to religion, and the need to love all religions. The purpose of the poem is to bring out the core aspects of any religion and to develop a love for all religions. The poem ends with the hope of having one mother religion, Humanity, which can unite all religions and make our world a humane region.

RELIGION

Why do we need religion?
Perhaps to be in a common region,
The community support we get,
Never allows us to forget.

Why objection when change of religion?
Perhaps the fear of contagion,
The benefit we get,
Never allows us to regret.

Why turmoil when insult to religion?
Perhaps the feeling of anti-religion,
The inner concern inculcated,
Never allows us to be manipulated.

Why religion is intrinsic to us?
Perhaps the sentiment is the focus,
The customs and traditions inherited,
Never allows us to be isolated.

Why many countries are secular?

Perhaps to be inclusive in particular,

The unity achieved in harmonious living,

Never allows us for separate living.

In the end, why love all religions?

Perhaps to form humane regions,

The sense of humanity to be hived,

Never allows us to be deprived.

PEBBLE 6: CHAYA – THE SOFTWARE ENGINEER

The poem describes the tenure of software engineers from the time of joining an organization until the time they leave. The poem recognizes the effort of software engineers in terms of extended work hours, responding at odd hours, learning new concepts, and incorporating frequent changes in their software. The purpose of the poem is to bring out the work cycle of a software engineer and describe the stages of software implementation.

CHAYA — THE SOFTWARE ENGINEER

You joined, at the scheduled time,

New project, environment, friends,

You adapted quickly, in record time,

At work, you believed on time.

I requested work at extended time,

Till 10 pm, 2 am, 4 am,

You never said "No", at all times,

At work, you believed on time.

I called at odd times,

Early morning, late evening, midnight,

You responded, in no time,

At work, you believed on time.

I explained the terms several times,

Provision, allocation, release, expenditure,

You listened patiently, every time,

At work, you believed on time.

I changed requirements multiple times,

Design, develop, merge, deploy,

You did it, with no extension of time,

At work, you believed on time.

I saw you last time,

In, out, up, down,

You were tired, this time,

At work, finally, you were relieved on time.

Thank you, Chaya, keep in touch at all times.

PEBBLE 7: ROOT CAUSE

It is very common to hear of cost escalations, corruption, disruption, devastation, unemployment, tension, and impatience. An attempt has been made to identify the cause and effect of incidents. The poem tries to give an account of incidents, their likely effect, and the probable root cause. The poem is meant to be thought-provoking with a bit of an analytical touch.

ROOT CAUSE

Delays, Non-Compliances, Deviations,

The effect would be cost escalations,

The root-cause, probably, is unplanned variations.

Degradation, Contamination, Pollution,

The effect would be high medication,

The root-cause, probably, is unhealthy implementation.

Preferences, Influences, Recommendations,

The effect would be corruption,

The root-cause, probably, is inefficient administration.

Rallies, Protests, Demonstrations,

The effect would be disruptions,

The root-cause, probably, is improper decisions.

War, Assault, Confrontation,

The effect would be devastation,

The root-cause, probably, is vengeful discrimination.

Illiteracy, Unskilled, Disengagement,

The effect would be unemployment,

The root-cause, probably, is poor management.

Pressure, Deadlines, Oppression,

The effect would be high tension,

The root-cause, probably, is quick ascension.

Anger, Hatred, Vengeance,

The effect would be impatience,

The root-cause, probably, is ego prominence.

PEBBLE 8: THE CHANGE

"Change" is a very common aspect of life. It can involve raising a child, education, profession, practicing traditions, society, government, and use of technologies. The poem attempts to address each of these aspects and mentions the possible results if changes are incorporated. The purpose of the poem is to identify the changes in various stages of life and how they would affect a person.

THE CHANGE

The way by which we are raised,
It is multi-factor based,
What if, the way is changed,
The outlook gets changed.

The framework in which we are educated,
It is designed to be deep-rooted,
What if, the framework is changed,
The perspective gets changed.

The industry in which we are engaged,
It is difficult to be gauged,
What if, the industry is changed,
The skillset gets changed.

The technology to which we are exposed,
It is science imposed,
What if, the technology is changed,
The mindset gets changed.

The tradition to which we are subjected,

It is very much time-tested,

What if, the tradition is changed,

The thinking gets changed.

The society to which we are bonded,

It is a norm surrounded,

What if, society is changed,

The living gets changed.

The system by which we are governed,

It is complex to be learned,

What if, the system is changed,

The behavior gets changed.

PEBBLE 9: POSITIVE MINDSET

It is very common to be advised to have a positive attitude and mindset. A positive mindset is an attribute of an individual based on various situations. Having a positive mindset in one situation does not guarantee the same in another situation. The poem involves describing various areas of failure and suggests ways to maintain a positive mindset. The purpose of the poem is to motivate the reader to analyze each situation and develop a positive mindset for a better life.

POSITIVE MINDSET

Could not cross the hurdle,

Did not know how to face the idle,

Thought about it in peace,

Going forward, I decided to surpass it at ease.

Could not maintain the friendship,

Did not know how to confront hardship,

Thought about it in isolation,

Going forward, I decided to build a strong relation.

Could not complete on time,

Did not know how to be in prime,

Thought about it in variation,

Going forward, I decided to transform with perfection.

Could not express my love,

Did not know how to be hand in glove,

Thought about it with an open heart,

Going forward, I decided to extend my kind heart.

Could not reach my target,

Did not know how it can be met,

Thought about it in deep concentration,

Going forward, I decided to achieve it in orchestration.

Could not become rich,

Did not know how to find the glitch,

Thought about it in stealth,

Going forward, I decided to sustain the focus on wealth.

Could not achieve my dream,

Did not know how to remain in cream,

Thought about it day and night,

Going forward, I decided to perspire till I get the light.

Failure does not mean it is not good,

Did not know how to feel good,

Thought about the ways to prevent,

Going forward, I decided to view it as means to reinvent.

THANK YOU

I would like to thank you very much for reading the poems and connecting yourself with them. Your time and effort are greatly appreciated. These poems can further be analyzed and customized to your frame of mind, which when done, can enhance the quality of your life.

Wishing you all the very best.

* 9 7 9 8 8 8 7 4 9 8 6 2 1 *